W9-COJ-455

SCHOLASTIC

Fluency
LESSONS
for the Overhead

GRADES
2–3

by Alyse Sweeney

NEW YORK • TORONTO • LONDON • AUCKLAND • SYDNEY **Teaching** *Resources*
MEXICO CITY • NEW DELHI • HONG KONG • BUENOS AIRES

For Jill

"Spider" from *Animals Nobody Loves* by Seymour Simon. Copyright © 2001 by Seymour Simon. Reprinted by permission of Chronicle Books.

"Twist and Turn!" from *Weather or Not* by Maryann Dobeck. Copyright © 2002 by Maryann Dobeck. Reprinted by permission of Scholastic Inc.

Excerpt from *One and One Is Too Much* by Daniel Ahearn. Copyright © 2002 by Daniel Ahearn. Reprinted by permission of Scholastic Inc.

"Untitled Chant" from *Writing Funny Bone Poems* by Paul Janeczko. Copyright © 2001 by Paul Janeczko. Reprinted by permission of Scholastic Inc.

"Eyeballs for Sale!" from *A Pizza the Size of the Sun* by Jack Prelutsky. Copyright © 1996 by Jack Prelutsky. Reprinted by permission of HarperCollins.

"What If?" by Helen H. Moore from *A Poem a Day.* Copyright © 2000 by Helen H. Moore. Reprinted by permission of Scholastic Inc.

"Mix-Up" by Andrea Martin from *Kids' Poems: Teaching Third & Fourth Graders to Love Writing Poetry* by Regie Routman. Copyright © 2000 by Regie Routman. Reprinted by permission of Regie Routman.

Excerpt from *Hey, Little Ant* by Phillip and Hannah Hoose. Copyright © 1998 by Phillip and Hannah Hoose. Reprinted by permission of Tricycle Press.

Excerpt from *Listening to Whales Sing* by Faith McNulty. Copyright © 1996 by Faith McNulty. Reprinted by permission of Scholastic Inc.

"At the Laundry" from *Poems to Count On* by Sandra Liatsos. Copyright © 1995 Sandra Liatsos. Reprinted by permission of Scholastic Inc.

Excerpt from *Alligator Baby* by Robert Munsch. Copyright © 1997 by Robert Munsch Enterprises, Ltd. Reprinted by permission of Scholastic Canada, Ltd.

"A Writing Tip From Jane Yolen" by Jane Yolen from Scholastic News. Edition 2 (2001). Copyright © 2001 by Scholastic Inc. Reprinted by permission of Scholastic Inc.

"Togetherness Chant" by Helen H. Moore from *A Poem a Day.* Copyright © 2000 by Helen H. Moore. Reprinted by permission of Scholastic Inc.

Excerpt from *Swamp Monster in Third Grade* by Debbie Dadey. Copyright © 2002 by Debbie Dadey. Reprinted by permission of Scholastic Inc.

"Mighty Midgets" from *Flies Taste With Their Feet: Weird Facts About Insects* by Melvin and Gilda Berger. Copyright © 1997 by Melvin and Gilda Berger. Reprinted by permission of Scholastic Inc.

Scholastic Inc. grants teachers permission to photocopy the transparencies and reproducible pages from this book for classroom use. No other part of this publication may be reproduced in whole or in part, or stored in a retrieval system, or transmitted in any form or by any means, electronic, mechanical, photocopying, recording, or otherwise, without written permission of the publisher. For information regarding permission, write to Scholastic Inc., 557 Broadway, New York, NY 10012.

Cover design by Maria Lilja
Interior design by Sydney Wright

Product ISBN: 0-439-58852-9
Book ISBN: 0-439-58855-3
Copyright © 2004 by Alyse Sweeney
Published by Scholastic Inc.
All rights reserved. Printed in the U.S.A.

5 6 7 8 9 10   40   13 12 11 10 09 08 07 06

Contents

Introduction

Direct and explicit. As with all areas of reading instruction, direct and explicit is the name of the game when it comes to fluency instruction. When you model for students how text should sound when read aloud, you help them enormously. But when you talk about *why* you emphasize particular words or phrases, read at varying speeds, and clump certain words together, students learn that meaning is carried not only by the words, but by the way the reader interprets and expresses the words.

What Is Fluency?

Fluency is the ability to read text accurately and effortlessly at an appropriate rate and with meaningful phrasing and intonation. Students who lack fluency read in a choppy, word-by-word manner. This lack of fluency is directly related to poor comprehension (Nathan and Stanovich, 1991). Some students who lack fluency spend most of their energy decoding words, leaving them with little energy for comprehending. Readers must have automatic recognition of words in order to read them in context and relate them to background knowledge so comprehension can take place (Snow, Burns, Griffin, 1998). Other students read words accurately, but their poor phrasing and intonation hampers their comprehension; it is often the phrases, versus individual words, that hold meaning (Rasinski, 2003).

Maryanne Wolf and Tami Katzir-Cohen (2001) have further defined fluency as a developmental process that involves all the components of reading acquisition, including phonemic awareness and decoding skills, as well as a strong vocabulary, knowledge of grammatical functions, and knowledge of word roots and parts. This definition moves away from the notion that fluency is an outcome that can be improved upon once the child already knows how to read. Rather, it supports the idea of making explicit fluency instruction a part of reading instruction from the very beginning. Wolf and Katzier-Cohen advocate teaching fluency at the letter pattern and word level. For instance, we can teach students to recognize chunks automatically (for example, -*an*) and have them practice reading word family words quickly (*can, man, pan*, etc.).

Fluency Instruction Makes Its Way Into Classrooms

Until recently, fluency instruction was largely ignored. In fact, Richard Allington (1983) described fluency as "the most neglected" skill in reading. Today, fluency is viewed as a critical component of reading instruction and of a child's reading development. The report of the National Reading Panel (2000) addresses the important role of fluency in reading instruction and many states and curriculum guidelines now include oral reading fluency as one of the many measures used in literacy assessment. This focus on fluency is indeed justified. A large-scale study by the National Assessment of Educational Progress (Pinnell et al., 1995) found that 44 percent of fourth graders did not have the level of fluency needed to comprehend on grade level.

Fluency Terms

phrasing—the way words are chunked together, marked by pauses

rate—the speed at which we read

intonation—the emphasis given to particular words or phrases

Building Fluency With Fluency Lessons for the Overhead: Grades 2–3

A Look at Each Lesson

Fluency Lessons for the Overhead: Grades 2–3 is a collection of 15 lessons. Each lesson has these elements: a student page with a carefully selected reading passage and a "Fun With Fluency" activity; an overhead transparency with the reading passage on it; and a teacher page, with a four-part instructional guide that incorporates best practices in fluency instruction. The instruction is organized into the following four components:

* a focus on comprehension ("Meaning First" component that focuses attention on the author's intended meaning; this focus continues through the "Model and Discuss Fluency" component)
* modeling ("Model and Discuss Fluency" component)
* guided practice ("All Together Now" component)
* independent practice ("Practice, Practice, Practice!" component)

The reading passages include poems and excerpts from both popular fiction and nonfiction. These passages are provided in two formats—as both transparencies and as blackline student reproducibles. The varied formats offer you several options for instructional presentation. For instance, the transparencies can serve as a powerful tool for modeling fluency because students can easily view the text as you read it aloud and point out the features that give clues to how to read. The transparencies are also a time-saver, allowing you to spend more time on instruction, and less time on lesson preparation. The reproducibles include a copy of the reading passages, which provides each student with opportunities for independent reading practice. In addition, the reproducibles provide a "Fun With Fluency" activity that reinforces fluency concepts presented in the lesson and extends students' comprehension of the passage.

Lesson Walk-Through To help you better envision the elements of each lesson and its intended use, see the diagrammatic "walk-through" lesson on pages 6 and 7.

Each fluency lesson begins with a read aloud and discussion of the passage. Use the discussion questions provided, or create your own, to help students focus on the meaning of the passage before exploring the fluency topics.

The fluency spotlight highlights the fluency element(s) that are the focus of the lesson. Feel free to draw students' attention to other fluency elements as you see fit.

The lesson proceeds to a script that serves as a guide for a modeled reading of the passage. Here, invite students to listen carefully to *how* you read the text—ideally from the transparency of the passage so that students can easily follow along as you point to and discuss the text. The goal is to keep the instruction direct and explicit as you explain *why* you read the text the way you do.

This section provides an assisted reading activity where students take part in the reading. The variety of echo and choral reading activities help students attain fluency with the passage alongside a fluent reader— the teacher, an other adult, or even a fluent student. Again, the transparency is an effective tool for helping students follow along and make the connection between how written words and special text features look and the way the words sound when read aloud. The assisted reading activities can take place multiple times over the days following the modeled reading for reinforcement and practice.

The variety of activities in this section provide opportunities for students to practice reading the passage, either independently or with partners. Several activities culminate in a reading performance. As with the assisted reading activities, these activities can be repeated as necessary for reinforcement.

Reading Passage E: "Eyeballs for Sale!"

FLUENCY SPOTLIGHT

PART 2
The Power of Punctuation

Exclamation Points

MEANING FIRST

Before the modeled reading, read aloud and discuss the poem. Pose these or other comprehension questions: *Where do the eyeballs come from? According to the poem, what does one do with the eyeballs? How do you know?* Now continue with the lesson and read the poem again with a focus on fluency.

MODEL AND DISCUSS FLUENCY

Proceed with a modeled reading of "Eyeballs for Sale!" stressing the excitement and energy with your voice when you read the exclamations. Use the script provided here as a sample for your own instructional dialogue with students.

"Exclamation points let the reader know that the sentence should be read with strong feelings of excitement, joy, fear, anger, horror, or surprise. Listen as I read the first two exclamations: Eyeballs for sale! Fresh eyeballs for sale! Can you tell which feeling the exclamation points highlight? Now listen as I read the same sentences as if they ended in periods. What was different about the two readings? Which reading do you prefer? Which reading sounds more natural?"

ALL TOGETHER NOW

Have children pretend they are street vendors with baskets full of fresh eyeballs to sell. in your best salesman voice, lead the choral reading of the poem, pointing to each word as the class follows along.

Practice, Practice, Practice!

Poetry Reading: After you model fluency with "Eyeballs for Sale!" have students practice reading the poem with the same phrasing, rate, and intonation. Then assign a time over the next week for each student to read the poem to the class. For example, have three students read the poem during morning meeting, two read it after lunch, and three read it at the close of the day.

24

Each reproducible page contains a student copy of the reading passage. The passage is to be used with the reading activity in the "Practice, Practice, Practice!" section, as well as with other rereading opportunities that you create. Encourage students to take the reading passages home with them and read to family members for additional practice.

Name: _____ Date: _____

Eyeballs for Sale!

(from *A Pizza the Size of the Sun* by Jack Prelutsky)

Eyeballs for sale!
Fresh eyeballs for sale!
Delicious, nutritious,
not moldy or stale.
Eyeballs from manticores,
ogres, and elves,
fierce dragon eyeballs
that cook by themselves.

Eyeballs served cold!
Eyeballs served hot!
If you like eyeballs,
then this is the spot.
Ladle a glassful,
a bowlful, or pail—
Eyeballs! Fresh eyeballs!
Fresh eyeballs for sale!

Fun With Fluency

1. How many exclamation points are in "Eyeballs for Sale!"?

_____

2. Why do you think the author used so many exclamation points?

_____
_____
_____
_____
_____

3. How do you think this poem would sound if there were no exclamation points? Explain your answer on the back of this page.

Fluency Lessons for the Overhead: Grades 2–3 Scholastic Teaching Resources, page 25

"Fun With Fluency" is an activity that reinforces the fluency element(s) of the lesson. The activities can be done as a class or individually, and some activities call for work with a partner. Always walk students through the directions and questions, and clarify any challenging vocabulary before they begin. Depending on your schedule and students' needs, the activity can be completed after you model and discuss the passage, or later in the week to provide more opportunities for repeated readings of the passage and to reinforce the fluency focus.

An Overview of the Book

Part 1: Phrasing, Rate, and Intonation In Part 1 of this book, students learn the three components of reading fluency: phrasing, rate, and intonation. They learn to think about what they read and have the author's intended meaning guide them to clump words together, emphasize certain words, and determine how quickly or slowly to read the text. Students also learn that the more they practice reading aloud a text, the smoother and more natural the words sound.

Part 2: The Power of Punctuation In Part 2, students learn that punctuation marks serve as signals. Each of the four poems highlights a particular punctuation mark that indicates to readers when to pause, when to emphasize words and read with emotion, when to raise their voice to indicate a question, or when to speak in another character's voice. The goal of this section is to help students understand that punctuation communicates how the author wants us to read the text. Acknowledging punctuation in text also helps us read the words in a natural manner, as if we were speaking.

Part 3: Putting It All Together Part 3 includes eight reading passages and poems in which students encounter a variety of punctuation and typographical signals. Modeled reading of the texts demonstrates several moods, sentence structures, and rhythms. As you explore the passages, talk explicitly about clues in the text that indicate how the words should sound when read aloud. Review and hand out the Fluent Reading Checklist on page 31. Encourage students to refer to the list when they feel their oral reading lacks expression and fluency or when they want to be sure to accurately communicate the author's meaning.

Appendix: Phrased Text Lessons The three Phrased Text Lessons (PTL) found in the Appendix are designed for students who regularly read in a word-by-word manner. These students are not grouping words into meaningful phrases, and therefore, their comprehension is weak. The step-by-step Phrased Text Lesson outlined by Rasinski (2003) provides explicit instruction in chunking words into meaningful segments with actual cues, or slashes, that are incorporated in the text and signal the reader when to pause.

How Fluency Lessons for the Overhead: Grades 2–3 Reflects Best Instructional Practices

Rasinski (2003) has identified effective instructional methods for teaching fluency:

Model fluent reading. When you model fluent reading and explain *why* you emphasize particular words or phrases, read at varying speeds, and clump certain words together, students learn the importance of acknowledging typographical features and interpreting the author's words.

- *Fluency Lessons for the Overhead* includes a sample script ("Model and Discuss Fluency" component) that serves as a framework for modeling an aspect of fluency and discussing the given reading passage.

Provide oral support for readers. Fluency and comprehension improve when students simultaneously read and listen to a fluent rendition of the text. There are several forms of supported reading, including choral reading and echo reading.

- *Fluency Lessons for the Overhead* suggests a guided practice activity (the "All Together Now" activity) with each lesson.

Provide opportunities for independent practice. Like all skills, practice is essential for fluency. It is well documented that repeated reading leads to improved fluency. With each reading, the reader's focus shifts from the mechanics of decoding to interpreting the words and applying the appropriate phrasing and intonation.

- *Fluency Lessons for the Overhead* pairs each reading passage with a motivating oral reading activity and stresses independent practice ("Practice, Practice, Practice!" activity).

Focus instruction on meaningful phrasing. In addition to being able to decode quickly and effortlessly, fluent readers use pauses to break text into meaningful chunks. Meaning often lies in the phrases of a text, rather than in individual words.

- *Fluency Lessons for the Overhead* explicitly addresses phrasing throughout the book and provides three phrased text lessons (Appendix, page 50).

Provide text written at the reader's independent reading level. Independent level text is relatively easy for the reader, who reads with 95 percent success (no more than roughly 1 in 20 difficult words).

- *Fluency Lessons for the Overhead* includes poems, fiction, and nonfiction reading passages written at varying levels of difficulty to meet the needs of students.

In his foreword found in *The Fluent Reader* (Rasinski, 2003), James Hoffman encourages teachers to tightly incorporate comprehension into fluency instruction.

- *Fluency Lessons for the Overhead* begins each lesson with an oral reading that first and foremost addresses the meaning of the passage ("Meaning First"). Only then does the teacher dive into the fluency lesson. Additionally, the "Model and Discuss Fluency" section consistently addresses the author's intended meaning and the ways in which the author communicates this intended meaning.

Tips for Using *Fluency Lessons for the Overhead*

* The fluency lessons are appropriate for individual, small group, or whole class lessons.

* Ideally, the modeling, guided reading, and independent reading practice take place over several days, for about twenty to thirty minutes a day.

* The book is set up in three parts. Part 2 builds on information from Part 1, and Part 3 builds on information from Part 2. However, within each part, there is no recommended sequence to follow. You can select the passages based on the reading passage topic, genre, or the fluency focus listed at the top of each lesson.

* Each reading passage comes in the form of a transparency and student reproducible. It may be more manageable for students to read off the transparency while you model reading the passage and during the guided practice. Remember to run a pointer under the words as you read them so students can keep their place. Hand out the student reproducible page when students are ready for the independent reading activity in the "Practice, Practice, Practice!" section.

* Keep comprehension in the forefront of fluency instruction and share with students the goal of fluency instruction—to increase comprehension by reading smoothly, accurately, and with expression.

* Send the reproducible reading passages home with students so they can practice and read for family members.

"Fluency is a wonderful bridge to comprehension and to a lifelong love of reading."
—Maryanne Wolf

PART 1
Phrasing, Rate, and Intonation
An Introduction

Effective fluency instruction, like all reading instruction, is direct and explicit. If the goal is for students to read with fluency, students need to understand and verbalize what a fluent reader does. Below are three mini-lessons that explain three components of fluency: proper phrasing, rate, and intonation. It is not important that students know these terms, only what they mean. The sample sentence below and the following three reading passages have little punctuation and typographical signals to demonstrate that our interpretation of the words and our knowledge of speech patterns guides us when we read.

Write the following sentence on the chalkboard or chart paper: Matt loves spaghetti and meatballs.

Phrasing is the way words are chunked together, marked by pauses.
First read the sentence in a word-by-word manner. Ask students how the sentence sounded. Explain that fluent readers chunk or group words together and use slight pauses between the clusters of words to make the reading sound more natural, like talking. Read the sentence with meaningful phrasing (*Matt loves / spaghetti and meatballs*). Talk about how some words sound natural *squished* together without a pause, like *spaghetti and meatballs*, *peanut butter and jelly* and *birthday cake*.

Rate is the speed at which we read.
Read the sentence slowly and monotone. Then read it at a natural speed. Do students hear the difference in the way the sentence was read? Which way did they like you to read it? Explain that fluent readers read at a speed similar to talking. The more they practice reading a particular text, the more natural and smooth they will sound. Let students know that the goal is not to read as quickly as possible, but to read at a natural speaking rate. Sometimes, however, the text makes more sense when read slowly or quickly. For example, *Hurry! Everybody hide or we'll ruin the surprise!* is best read quickly, while, *Slowly, the snail slithered down, down, down the window* is best read slowly.

Intonation is the emphasis given to particular words or phrases.
As you read the sentence, emphasize a different word each time, pointing to that word as you read.

   1. **Matt** loves spaghetti and meatballs.

   2. Matt **loves** spaghetti and meatballs.

   3. Matt loves spaghetti and **meatballs**.

Did students hear the difference in the way the sentence was read? Talk about how emphasizing different words changes the focus in the sentence. In version 1, we are meant to focus on the fact that it is Matt, and not someone else, who loves this dish. In version 2, we are meant to understand that Matt is really, really fond of spaghetti and meatballs. In version 3, we are meant to focus on the fact that it is spaghetti and meatballs, rather than spaghetti without meatballs that Matt finds delicious.

FLUENCY SPOTLIGHT

PART 1

Phrasing, Rate, and Intonation

Phrasing, Rate, and Intonation

MEANING FIRST

Before the modeled reading, read aloud and discuss the passage. Pose this or another comprehension question: *What message about spiders is the author trying to pass on to the reader?* Now continue with the lesson and read the text again with a focus on fluency.

MODEL AND DISCUSS FLUENCY

Proceed with a modeled reading of "Spider" that is smooth and expressive. Use the script provided here as a sample for your own instructional dialogue with students.

Phrasing: *"When we speak, we naturally clump words together within a sentence. Listen as I group certain words together in this sentence:* **They are afraid / that spiders will jump up / and bite them.** *Do you hear how* **jump up** *and* **bite them** *naturally go together? Listen to how awkward the sentence sounds when I pause after every word:* **They / are / afraid / that / spiders / will / jump / up / and / bite / them.//**

Rate: *"Notice that I read this passage at a natural speed—not particularly fast or slow. I read as if I were talking to all of you about spiders."*

Intonation: *"When we speak, and also when we read fluently, we naturally emphasize certain words. For example, listen to the word I emphasize in this sentence:* **Many people think spiders are** <u>**horrible**</u> **creatures.** *I put more stress on the word* **horrible** *to add drama to the sentence and because the word* **horrible** *sounds more horrible when stretched out and spoken in such a way. When we emphasize certain words, we help communicate the author's intended meaning and make Read-Alouds more interesting to listen to."*

ALL TOGETHER NOW

Point to each word as you do a choral reading of "Spider." Explain that this text has little punctuation to tell the reader which words to clump together, which words to emphasize, or how fast or slow to read. It is up to the reader to think about what they are reading and decide how it would sound the most natural.

Practice, Practice, Practice!

Partner Reading: For partners of the same ability, have one student read "Spider" three times to a partner and receive feedback. Partners then switch roles. For partners of different abilities, pair above-level readers with on-level readers and on-level readers with below-level readers. First, the stronger reader models fluent reading with a paragraph or the entire passage. As the less fluent reader reads the same text aloud, the fluent reader provides assistance when needed. The less fluent reader rereads the text until he or she can read it accurately and with fluency.

Name: _____   Date: _____

Spider

(from *Animals Nobody Loves* by Seymour Simon)

Many people think spiders are horrible creatures. They are afraid that spiders will jump up and bite them. Some people run away when they see a spider. Others try to kill any spider they see.

But spiders do not normally bite human beings. Spiders usually trap insects they prey upon—from flies and mosquitoes to grasshoppers and crickets—in beautiful silken webs. Then they bite the insect and inject a poison to quiet it down so that they can eat it. So we should remember that spiders do us a lot of good by getting rid of insect pests.

Fun With Fluency

1. How did you feel about spiders before reading this passage?

_____

_____

2. Did the author make you feel any differently about spiders? Explain your answer. _____

_____

3. Find a sentence from the text above that has a word or words that you would emphasize when reading aloud. Underline the word or words.

_____

_____

Explain why emphasizing the word or words would make sense.

_____

FLUENCY SPOTLIGHT

Phrasing, Rate, and Intonation

MEANING FIRST

Before the modeled reading, read aloud and discuss the passage. Pose this or another comprehension question: *How does a tornado sound, look, and feel?* Now continue with the lesson and read the text again with a focus on fluency.

MODEL AND DISCUSS FLUENCY

Proceed with a modeled reading of "Twist and Turn!" making it sound dramatic. Use the script provided here as a sample for your own instructional dialogue with students.

Phrasing: *"Sometimes authors use a series of short sentences, followed by a long sentence, to add drama to the text and make it sound more interesting. Listen to the way I exaggerate the pauses after each short sentence in the first paragraph. When I pause for an extra moment before reading the next sentence, I hope to build suspense for the listener."*

Rate: *"When you read aloud, remember to pay attention to the meaning of the words. Think about how you think those words would be spoken. In "Twist and Turn!," the author describes something that is spectacular and dramatic. She chooses her words carefully and uses short sentences to draw attention to those words. I can imagine that if she were here reading this text to us, she might read these short sentences in a somewhat slow and deliberate way. If they are read too quickly, the reader may not have enough time to visualize each fabulous detail. Listen as I read the sentences again and notice that I am taking my time so the words can sink in:* **The sky grows dark. There is a big thunderstorm. Lightning flashes. Thunder roars. Rain and hail pour down.***"*

Intonation: *"When we draw attention to certain words, we pay even more attention to their meaning. Listen to the word I choose to emphasize in this sentence:* **When it hits the ground, it sweeps away everything in its path.** *I stressed the word* **everything** *to draw attention to the power of a tornado."*

ALL TOGETHER NOW

Begin with an echo reading of "Twist and Turn!" Read with clear phrasing and dramatic intonation, pointing to the words on the overhead as the class reads aloud. Then move into a choral reading of the text. After several choral readings, invite students to read the passage aloud with appropriate phrasing, rate, and intonation.

Practice, Practice, Practice!

Tape-Assisted Reading: Tape-assisted reading is a motivating way for students to build fluency. Begin by creating a tape of "Twist and Turn!" You may want to have other adults or fluent readers create the tape to give students a variety of voices to listen to. First, students listen to the passage on tape, pointing to the words on their hard copy as they follow along. Students then read aloud with the tape, as they would in choral reading. Provide a purpose for students to practice and perform by inviting them to make their own tape of the reading passage. Challenge them to see how close they can make their version of the reading sound like the original taped reader. Perhaps their version can replace the original and serve as the new model for that reading passage!

Name: _____   Date: _____

Twist and Turn!

(from *Weather or Not* by Maryann Dobeck)

One of the worst storms is a tornado. The sky grows dark. There is a big thunderstorm. Lightning flashes. Thunder roars. Rain and hail pour down. A twisting funnel of high winds forms a tornado. When it hits the ground, it sweeps away everything in its path.

The winds in a tornado may reach 300 miles per hour. That's the fastest wind on Earth. The roaring wind sounds like a train.

Fun With Fluency

1. There are often many ways to read a sentence with expression. In a soft voice, read aloud this sentence and emphasize the word **fastest**.

That's the **fastest** wind on Earth.

Now read the sentence again. This time emphasize the words **on Earth**.

That's the fastest wind **on Earth**.

Did both readings sound natural? _____

2. What meaning are you trying to get across to the listener when you read the sentence emphasizing **fastest**?

_____

_____

3. What meaning are you trying to get across to the listener when you read the sentence emphasizing **on Earth**?

_____

_____

FLUENCY SPOTLIGHT

Phrasing, Rate, and Intonation

MEANING FIRST

Before the modeled reading, read aloud and discuss the passage. Pose these or other comprehension questions: *How does Julie feel about being in the waiting room with her mom? How do you know?* Now continue with the lesson and read the text again with a focus on fluency.

MODEL AND DISCUSS FLUENCY

Proceed with a modeled reading of *One and One Is Too Much*, using your voice to express Julie's boredom and uneasiness. Use the script provided here as a sample for your own instructional dialogue with students.

Phrasing: *"Reading with fluency sounds a lot like the way people speak. When we talk, we naturally squish certain words together. For instance, we wouldn't say to someone,* **I am / kind / of excited / for winter / to arrive** *(emphasize the pause before and after the word* kind.*) The words* **kind of** *naturally go together. Listen to the way I clump words together in this sentence from the passage:* **Julie / was kind of / excited about / the new baby."**

Rate: *"When you read aloud, how do you know how fast or slow to read? One way is to think about the meaning of the words you read. For example, if you are reading the play-by-play of an exciting basketball game, you might read quickly, the way a sports announcer speaks quickly to keep up with the action. In this passage, the character Julie is waiting in a doctor's office, looking at a clock on the wall. That's why I read the passage using a slow, relaxed speed."*

Intonation: *"Listen as I read this sentence from the passage and tell me which word I emphasized:* **Julie** <u>**hated**</u> **waiting at a doctor's office, even when her mom was the patient.** *I emphasized the word* **hated** *because that word carries a lot of emotion and feeling. When I read an emotional word with feeling, the sentence comes alive, and in this case, Julie's feelings seem more real."*

ALL TOGETHER NOW

Do a choral reading of *One and One Is Too Much*, pointing to each word as you read. Emphasize the pauses between sentences and the rhythm the author creates with a balance of short and long sentences. Explain that this reading passage has very little punctuation to tell the reader which words to clump together, which words to emphasize, or how fast or slow to read. It is up to the reader to think about what they are reading and decide how it would sound the most natural.

Practice, Practice, Practice!

Divide the class into groups of three and assign each member a number from one to three. The *ones* read aloud the first three sentences of the passage. The *twos* read the remainder of the first paragraph, and the *threes* read the second paragraph. Have the students draw a small star beside the fourth sentence in the first paragraph and the first word of the second paragraph to indicate the reading parts. The partners provide support to each other when needed and swap reading parts once they agree that each member has read their portion with fluency. When they are finished, each partner will have had a turn reading the three segments of the passage.

Name: _____   Date: _____

Excerpt from One and One Is Too Much
by Daniel Ahearn

Julie looked at the clock on the wall. She flipped through a magazine. Julie hated waiting at a doctor's office, even when her mom was the patient. There wasn't anything interesting to read. The chairs were uncomfortable. She couldn't help staring at the other women who were there. She wondered if they were all going to have babies like her mom.

Julie was kind of excited about the new baby. Something was bothering her about it, too. She wasn't sure what it was.

Fun With Fluency

In a soft voice, read the sentences below. For each pair of sentences, underline the words in bold that sound natural "squished" together.

Example:
Julie looked at the clock **on the wall**.
Julie looked at the **clock on** the wall.

1.
The **chairs were** uncomfortable.
The chairs **were uncomfortable**.

2.
Julie **was kind** of excited about the new baby.
Julie was **kind of** excited about the new baby.

3.
She wasn't sure **what it was**.
She wasn't sure **what it** was.

PART 2

The Power of Punctuation
An Introduction

The reading passages in Part 2 were selected to highlight the role punctuation plays in phrasing, rate, and intonation. Begin with a brief overview of punctuation marks and typographical signals and what they mean. Use the Punctuation and Signals Poster on page 21, or create your own larger version and have students fill in the chart. Students can also add to the chart as they encounter new signals.

Use the sentences below (or your own sentences) to demonstrate how punctuation and typographical signals affect meaning and provide clues for how to read text. Write the sentences on a chart.

I love spaghetti and meatballs.

I love spaghetti and meatballs!

I love spaghetti and meatballs?

I love spaghetti and MEATBALLS!

I <u>love</u> spaghetti and meatballs.

I love spaghetti and meatballs.

I love spaghetti (and meatballs)!

After you read each sentence, talk about how the signals affected how you read them. How did the meaning of the sentence change? Can students tell you how you should read a sentence you point to *before* you read it? Have volunteers take turns reading the sentences and explaining why they read the sentence as they did. Explain that paying attention to these signals not only makes a story more interesting, it also makes the story easier to understand because, as they now see, the signals help the reader interpret the author's words and their meaning.

Punctuation and Signals Poster

Punctuation and Signals	What do you do when you see it?	Example
,	Pause at a **comma**.	Kevin collects stamps, baseball cards, and comic books.
.	Pause a bit longer at a **period**.	Bats and elephants are mammals. Owls and geese are birds.
?	Raise your voice at the end of a sentence with a **question mark** to show you are asking a question or expressing doubt.	What is your favorite food? You stayed up all night?
!	Read a sentence ending in an **exclamation point** with strong feelings of joy, fear, anger, horror, or surprise.	She's coming! Hide before we ruin the surprise! I made five baskets in a row! Help! My foot is stuck!
" "	Read the words in **quotation marks** as you think the character or speaker might say them. Sometimes quotation marks are around individual words for emphasis.	"Don't dillydally all day," said the old woman. A "green" person is someone who loves nature.
. . .	Pause a bit longer at an **ellipsis**.	"I . . . I can't believe . . . Did I really win?" asked the girl.
—	Pause a bit longer at a **dash**.	This heat—108 degrees—is unbearable.
( )	Pause before and after a **parenthesis**.	The Wagner Playground (also known as the tire-swing playground) is on East Street.
Words written in special ways: *italics* **boldface** <u>underline</u> ALL CAPS	Stress these words.	"You ate *that*?" gasped Joe. "**Ooouch!** I've been stung by a bee!" shrieked Sue. "The ball goes <u>in</u> the hoop, not <u>over</u> it," sneered Rick. "HIP, HIP, HOORAY!" shouted the team.

FLUENCY SPOTLIGHT

PART 2

The Power of Punctuation

Commas

MEANING FIRST

Before the modeled reading, read aloud and discuss the chant. Pose this or another comprehension question: *Sometimes children recite chants like this one as they play jump rope. Why do you think that is?* Now continue with the lesson and read the chant again with a focus on fluency.

MODEL AND DISCUSS FLUENCY

Proceed with a modeled reading of the chant, emphasizing the rhythm. Use the script provided here as a sample for your own instructional dialogue with students.

"This chant, like all chants, has a definite rhythm. There are lots of commas in this chant that help create the rhythm. Commas are signals that remind the reader to take a brief pause. Notice in this chant that there is a comma in the same place on each line—in the middle of the line and at the end. As I read the chant again, I'm going to raise my hand each time I come to a comma. Listen to the way I pause each time. (With one hand, point to each word on the transparency as you read and raise the other hand at each comma.) In addition to letting us know when to pause, the commas also serve to cluster certain words together. Let's see what happens when I put commas in different places and read the chant. (With an overhead pen, stick commas in different spots or rewrite the sentences. For example, Ooo-ah wanna, piece, of pie, Pie too, sweet wanna piece of, meat). What happened to our rhythm? Remember that commas have an important job. They remind the reader to pause, and they group words together. As a result, they help sentences have a smooth and natural rhythm."

ALL TOGETHER NOW

Begin with a line-by-line echo reading of the chant. Point to each word on the transparency as the students follow along. Then divide the class in half and have the two groups alternately read each line (one group read the first line and the second group read the second line, etc.). Choral read the chant in this manner several times, emphasizing the pauses and the rhythm the pauses create. Try reading the chant with a clap at each comma. Encourage students to have fun with the chant, moving their heads and bodies to the rhythm of the words.

Practice, Practice, Practice!

Cross-Age Reading: Cross-age reading creates a wonderfully authentic reason to practice and perform. Have students practice choral reading the passage in small groups. When they have mastered the text, send each group into a different class of a lower grade to perform the chant. The performance can consist of reading the chant three times. Students can encourage their audience to join in with the clapping.

Name: _____   Date: _____

Untitled Chant

(from *Writing Funny Bone Poems* by Paul Janeczko)

Ooo-ah, wanna piece of pie,
Pie too sweet, wanna piece of meat,
Meat too tough, wanna ride a bus,
Bus was full, wanna ride a bull,
Bull too fat, want your money back,
Money too green, wanna jelly bean,
Jelly bean not cooked, wanna read a book,
Book not read, wanna go to bed.
So close your eyes and count to ten,
And if you miss, start all over again.

Fun With Fluency

Commas remind the reader to pause. They also group words together in a meaningful way. Below are lines from the chant. First add two commas in the <u>wrong</u> places. Read the sentence and notice how unnatural the line sounds. Then rewrite the line so the commas are in the correct place. Check your work with the chant above.

1. Ooo-ah wanna piece of pie

_____

2. Pie too sweet wanna piece of meat

_____

3. Meat too tough wanna ride a bus

_____

FLUENCY SPOTLIGHT

Exclamation Points

MEANING FIRST

Before the modeled reading, read aloud and discuss the poem. Pose these or other comprehension questions: *Where do the eyeballs come from? According to the poem, what does one do with the eyeballs? How do you know?* Now continue with the lesson and read the poem again with a focus on fluency.

MODEL AND DISCUSS FLUENCY

Proceed with a modeled reading of "Eyeballs for Sale!" stressing the excitement and energy with your voice when you read the exclamations. Use the script provided here as a sample for your own instructional dialogue with students.

"Exclamation points let the reader know that the sentence should be read with strong feelings of excitement, joy, fear, anger, horror, or surprise. Listen as I read the first two exclamations: **Eyeballs for sale! Fresh eyeballs for sale!** *Can you tell which feeling the exclamation points highlight? Now listen as I read the same sentences as if they ended in periods. What was different about the two readings? Which reading do you prefer? Which reading sounds more natural?"*

ALL TOGETHER NOW

Have children pretend they are street vendors with baskets full of fresh eyeballs to sell. In your best salesman voice, lead the choral reading of the poem, pointing to each word as the class follows along.

Practice, Practice, Practice!

Poetry Reading: After you model fluency with "Eyeballs for Sale!" have students practice reading the poem with the same phrasing, rate, and intonation. Then assign a time over the next week for each student to read the poem to the class. For example, have three students read the poem during morning meeting, two read it after lunch, and three read it at the close of the day.

Name: _____   Date: _____

Eyeballs for Sale!

(from *A Pizza the Size of the Sun* by Jack Prelutsky)

Eyeballs for sale!
Fresh eyeballs for sale!
Delicious, nutritious,
not moldy or stale.
Eyeballs from manticores,
ogres, and elves,
fierce dragon eyeballs
that cook by themselves.

Eyeballs served cold!
Eyeballs served hot!
If you like eyeballs,
then this is the spot.
Ladle a glassful,
a bowlful, or pail—
Eyeballs! Fresh eyeballs!
Fresh eyeballs for sale!

Fun With Fluency

1. How many exclamation points are in "Eyeballs for Sale!"?

   _____

2. Why do you think the author used so many exclamation points?

   _____

   _____

   _____

   _____

   _____

3. How do you think this poem would sound if there were no exclamation points? Explain your answer on the back of this page.

PART 2

The Power of Punctuation

Question Marks

MEANING FIRST

Before the modeled reading, read aloud and discuss the poem and talk about favorite lines. Can students explain how this poem is structured? (*list of opposites written in question form*) Have students brainstorm opposites and then share their own "What if?" questions. Now continue with the lesson and read the poem again with a focus on fluency.

MODEL AND DISCUSS FLUENCY

Proceed with a modeled reading of "What If?" emphasizing the rise in your voice after each question mark. Use the script provided here as a sample for your own instructional dialogue with students.

"Listen as I read the first stanza again. Notice how I raise my voice at the end of each sentence because they end in question marks. Now listen as I read the last stanza. My voice did not rise at the end of the last sentence because this sentence ends in an exclamation point. I read the last sentence with a lot of energy, but my voice didn't rise at the end."

ALL TOGETHER NOW

Do an echo reading of "What If?" to reinforce and emphasize the unique sound of questions. Read each question, pointing to the words on the transparency, and have the class read the question with the same phrasing and intonation. After several readings, reverse roles and have the class lead in the echo reading while you follow, or invite individuals to lead in the echo reading.

Practice, Practice, Practice!

Tape-Assisted Reading: Questions have a unique sound. Invite students to make a tape of their reading of "What If?" and listen to the rise in their voice when they read each question. Students should practice reading the poem and achieve fluency before taping the poem. For additional reinforcement, play the tapes back to the class. Is it clear each time the reader reads a question?

Name: _____   Date: _____

What If?

(by Helen H. Moore from *A Poem a Day*)

What if snowballs were hot?
What if water were dry?
What if parrots could swim,
and opossums could fly?
What if:
Teachers were kids?
Doctors never gave shots;
What if:
Cooks put the lids
underneath cooking pots?

What if:
Meanness were nice,
saying "thank you" was rude,
and your parents still thought
you should eat baby food?

If all good things were bad,
and all bad things were good,
the world would be different,
it certainly would—
Would you like it?
Not I—
I'd go out of my wits,
If I had to get used
To all these opposites!

Fun With Fluency

1. Put a check next to the line where the poet answers one of her own questions.

2. Choose a question from the poem to answer. Put a star next to the question. Then write an answer on the lines below.

   _____

   _____

   _____

   _____

   _____

   _____

3. Select a line from the poem to illustrate on the back of this page.

FLUENCY SPOTLIGHT

Quotation Marks

MEANING FIRST

Before the modeled reading, read aloud and discuss the poem. Pose these or other comprehension questions: *Do you ever feel mixed up about the same things the author of this poem wrote about? What are some examples of things that mix you up?* Now continue with the lesson and read the poem again with a focus on fluency.

MODEL AND DISCUSS FLUENCY

Proceed with a modeled reading of "Mix-Up," emphasizing the quotes from the various family members. Use the script provided here as a sample for your own instructional dialogue with students.

"Mix-Up" is a fun poem to read because it is filled with quotes from members of the poet's family. A quote is the actual words that a real person or character says. Quotation marks tell us that we are reading words that a real person or fictional character said. Listen to the way I read each quote. I read them as I think the mom, dad, sister, friend, or grandma might say them."

ALL TOGETHER NOW

Begin with an echo reading of the poem, pointing to the words on the transparency as the students follow along. Then read the lines of the poet, Andrea Martin, while the class reads the quotes from the family members, using the echo reading of the quotes as a model.

Practice, Practice, Practice!

Poetry Duet: Divide the class into pairs, matching fluent readers with less fluent readers. Have one partner read the part of the poet, Andrea Martin, while the other partner reads the quotes. Partners provide feedback and support to each other, and practice reading the poem as a duet until they are satisfied with their fluency. They can then perform "Mix-Up" for the class.

Name: _____   **Date:** _____

Mix-Up

(by Andrea Martin from Kids' Poems: Teaching Third & Fourth Graders to Love Writing Poetry)

Sometimes my mom mixes me up.
"Do this."
"Don't do that."
That mixes me up.

Sometimes my dad mixes me up.
"Wash the dishes."
"Help me."
"Come here."
"Never mind."
That always mixes me up.

Sometimes my sister mixes me up.
"Wash my gym clothes."
"Don't wash my gym clothes."
That mixes me up.

Sometimes my friends mix me up.
"You can use them."
"You can't use them."
That really mixes me up.

Sometimes my grandma mixes me up.
"Give me this."
"Give me that."
That mixes me up.

I'm all mixed up.

Fun With Fluency

1. Fill in the lines to create your own stanza to this poem.

Sometimes my

_____

mixes me up.

_____

_____

_____

_____

_____

That mixes me up.

2. Now read your stanza to a partner with expression and with two voices—yours and the person or people your stanza describes.

PART 3

Putting It All Together
An Introduction

In Part 1 of this book, students learn about phrasing, rate, and intonation with text that has very few punctuation marks or typographical signals. In Part 2 students learn that punctuation marks serve as signals and help communicate how the author wants us to read the text. Putting It All Together, the third part in this book, includes eight reading passages and poems in which students will encounter a variety of punctuation and typographical signals. Modeled readings of the texts demonstrate distinct moods, sentence structures, and rhythms. As you explore the passages, talk explicitly about clues in the text that indicate how the words should sound when read aloud. Review and hand out the Fluent Reading Checklist on page 31. Encourage students to refer to the list when they feel their oral reading lacks expression and fluency and they want to be sure they are accurately communicating the author's meaning.

Name: _____   Date: _____

Do You Do These Things When You Read?

☐ I think about the meaning of the words I read and how they would naturally sound when spoken.

☐ I make sure that what I am reading makes sense.

☐ I follow the rules of punctuation marks.

☐ I pay attention when words are written in an unusual way, such as all caps, boldface, italics, or words written very big or very small.

☐ When I read a rhyming poem or text, I emphasize the rhyming words.

☐ When I read dialogue, I read the words as I think the person or character would say them.

☐ I read at the same speed as I talk, not too slow and not too fast. But I read certain words quickly or slowly if it sounds more natural to read the words that way (for example, "Run! The bear is right behind you!").

FLUENCY SPOTLIGHT

Dialogue, Typographical Signals, Rhyming

MEANING FIRST

Before the modeled reading, read aloud and discuss the passage. Pose these or other comprehension questions: *How does this conversation between the kid and the ant make you feel? Have you ever thought about how the world looks through the eyes of an ant?* Now continue with the lesson and read the text again with a focus on fluency.

MODEL AND DISCUSS FLUENCY

Proceed with a modeled reading of the excerpt from *Hey, Little Ant*. Emphasize the different emotions of the kid and the ant. Use the script provided here as a sample for your own instructional dialogue with students.

Dialogue: *"I'm going to read a dialogue between two characters—a kid and an ant. Listen to the way I'll use a different tone of voice for each character. Did you hear the way I sounded like a bully when I read the kid's words? When I read the ant's words, I wanted the ant to sound terrified. This is the way I think the characters would sound if they were speaking the parts."*

Typographical Signals: *"Notice how the words **squish** and **please** are written in bold type. The author wants us to really emphasize these words and say them with a lot of energy. Can you hear the difference when I read the word **squish** in a normal voice and when I read **squish** with emphasis, as the author suggests?"* Read **Well now it's gonna squish you flat**, then **Well now it's gonna <u>squish</u> you flat**.

Rhyming: *"Here's a tip for making a poem sound smooth and rhythmic when you read it aloud: Stress the rhyming words. The rhyming words in the first stanza are **crack**, **back**, **that**, and **flat**. Listen as I emphasize these words when I read the stanza:* **Hey, little ant down in the <u>crack</u>, Can you hear me? Can you talk <u>back</u>?** *...These words seem to want to be read with a little more oomph, don't they?"*

ALL TOGETHER NOW

Have one side of the room read the part of the kid and the other side read the part of the ant. Choral read the text, emphasizing the menacing tone of the kid and the pleading tone of the ant. Also emphasize the rhyming words and words in boldface type.

Practice, Practice, Practice!

Cross-Age Reading: Begin by having partners each take a part and practice reading with each other. Then provide students with the book *Hey, Little Ant* or a copy of the full text. Read the text aloud several times with the students and follow up with a choral reading. Then have the partners perform the full text for a younger audience. In groups of four, have two students read the part of the kid and two students read the part of the ant.

Name: _____ Date: _____

Excerpt from **Hey, Little Ant**

by Phillip and Hannah Hoose

Kid: Hey, little ant down in the crack,
      Can you hear me? Can you talk back?
      See my shoe, can you see that?
      Well now it's gonna **squish** you flat.

Ant: Please, oh please, do not squish me,
      Change your mind and let me be,
      I'm on my way with a crumb of pie,
      Please, oh **please**, don't make me die!

Fun With Fluency

1. Underline a sentence that shows that the kid is a bully.

2. Underline a sentence that shows that the ant is scared.

3. In a soft voice, read the part of the kid as if he or she were scared.

Does it sound right? _____ Why or why not? _____

_____

4. In a soft voice, read the part of the ant as if it were a bully.

Does it sound right? _____ Why or why not? _____

_____

5. On the back of this page, describe the ending you would like

this story to have.

FLUENCY SPOTLIGHT

Pauses and Phrasing

MEANING FIRST

Before the modeled reading, read aloud and discuss the passage. Pose these or other comprehension questions: *What happens when a whale spouts? How do you feel after reading this passage?* Now continue with the lesson and read the passage again with a focus on fluency.

MODEL AND DISCUSS FLUENCY

Proceed with a modeled reading of the excerpt from *Listening to Whales Sing*. Emphasize the suspenseful tone and stress the pauses after each comma, dash, and semicolon. Use the script provided here as a sample for your own instructional dialogue with students.

"There are several types of punctuation that tell the reader to pause. This passage has three—the dash, the semi-colon, and the comma."

Dash: *"Listen as I read the second sentence:* **Almost beside me—a whale comes up and spouts.** *A dash signals the reader to pause a bit longer than a comma. Notice how this pause helps create drama and suspense. The author could have written,* **A whale comes up and spouts beside me,** *but the first way is more interesting."*

Semicolon: *"Let's look at the next sentence.* **I can see the blowhole on the top of its head; it opens as the whale breathes out—then in.** *The first punctuation mark that tells us to pause is a semicolon. Like the dash, the semicolon is a longer pause than a comma. Sometimes, a semicolon connects two sentences, like in this case."*

Dash: *"Look at the dash in this sentence . . .* **it opens as the whale breathes out—then in.** *This dash actually imitates the way a breath sounds: breathe in, pause, breathe out."*

Comma: *"The following sentence uses two commas:* **I can see its long, dark back and a flipper, shaped like the wing of an airplane.** *Listen as I slow down at each comma, giving you time to picture the details of the whale's back and flipper."*

ALL TOGETHER NOW

Do an echo reading of the passage, one sentence at a time. Emphasize the pauses and point to the words on the transparency as the students follow along.

Practice, Practice, Practice!

Tape-Assisted Reading: Begin by creating a tape of the excerpt from *Listening to Whales Sing*. Students listen to the passage on tape, pointing to the words on their copy as they follow along. Students then read aloud with the tape, as they would in choral reading. Provide a purpose for students to practice by inviting them to make their own tape of the reading passage. Encourage students to pay special attention to the variety of signals that indicate a pause. Remind students that pauses make text sound interesting and dramatic.

Name: _____   Date: _____

Excerpt from **Listening to Whales Sing**
by Faith McNulty

Suddenly it happens
almost beside me—a whale
comes up and spouts.

I can see the blowhole
on the top of its head;
it opens as the whale
breathes out—then in.
I can see its long, dark back
and a flipper, shaped like
the wing of an airplane.

I even think I glimpse an eye looking
right at me. My heart almost stops.
As the whale dives down again,
giant flukes rise from the water.
They look like the wings
of a huge butterfly.

The whale disappears.
The little boat rocks—
I lose my balance
and fall into cold, cold water.
I come up splashing and fighting
to get my breath.
I hear Jenny yelling for Kevin.
She is standing up in the boat, waving.
She throws a life ring into the water,
but it lands far away—out of my reach.

Fun With Fluency

For each sentence, put in commas where you think they are needed.

1. Sometimes I like to read before I fall asleep.

2. Do you like vanilla chocolate or strawberry ice cream best?

3. As I awoke this morning I heard a bird singing.

4. The girl stood smiled then took a bow.

5. The dog had long red hair and big spots.

FLUENCY SPOTLIGHT

Dialogue and Intonation, Commas Within Lists, Rhyme

MEANING FIRST

Before the modeled reading, read aloud and discuss the poem. Pose these or other comprehension questions: *Do any of you help with the laundry at home and sort the socks? Why is it more difficult for the caterpillar to sort the socks than it is for the katydid?* Now continue with the lesson and read the poem again with a focus on fluency.

MODEL AND DISCUSS FLUENCY

Proceed with a modeled reading of "At the Laundry." Emphasize the character's voice, the commas within the list, and the rhyming words. Use the script provided here as a sample for your own instructional dialogue with students.

Dialogue and Intonation: *"'At the Laundry' is a poem where two characters—a caterpillar and a katydid—talk to each other. Listen as I read the words, or the dialogue, of the caterpillar. I make the caterpillar sound upset and frustrated because he says he needs help sorting all his socks. Now let's compare the frustrated and overwhelmed tone of the caterpillar with the helpful and relaxed tone of the katydid:* **'Don't worry,' said the Katy-did, 'I'll help you sort them out — . . .'** *When you think about the meaning of these words, you realize that the katydid's tone of voice is going to be very different than that of the caterpillar."*

Commas Within Lists: *"Yellow socks, and orange socks, purple socks, and green. Red, and blue, and pink ones, too, and striped ones in-between. In these sentences, commas play the important role of separating items in a list. If you read the sentences without any commas, it would sound terrible—like a run-on sentence. The commas help separate each item so they don't all run into each other. The commas also give the sentence a nice rhythm."*

Rhyme: *"'At the Laundry' is a rhyming poem, which means we have the opportunity to emphasize the rhyming words when we read the poem aloud. Stressing the rhyming words in a poem gives the poem an easy flow and rhythm when read aloud:* **"My goodness!" said the caterpillar. "I am such a mixed-up <u>messer</u>! I need help to sort these socks—and put them neatly in my <u>dresser</u>."** *Which words should be emphasized in the remaining sentences of the poem?"*

ALL TOGETHER NOW

Divide the class into two groups. One group choral reads the caterpillar dialogue and the other group choral reads the katydid dialogue. Have students read along as you point to the words on the transparency. After a few readings, have the class switch parts.

Practice, Practice, Practice!

Partner Reading: After the class choral reading of "At the Laundry," partners can read from their student copies. Have each partner read the part of the caterpillar or the katydid, and switch parts when they feel they have reached a fluent level of reading. As always with partner reading, encourage students to gently support each other and offer guidance when needed.

Name: _____   Date: _____

At the Laundry
by Sandra Liatsos

"My goodness!" said the caterpillar.
"I am such a mixed-up messer!
I need help to sort these socks—
And put them neatly in my dresser.
Yellow socks, and orange socks,
Purple socks, and green.
Red, and blue, and pink ones, too,
and striped ones in-between.
I've put them in the washer
and I've put them in the dryer.
And now they're in a jumbled heap
that keeps on growing higher."

"Don't worry," said the Katy-did,
"I'll help you sort them out—
the reds with reds, the blues with blues
that's what it's all about.
We'll sort them all until
each color's standing in its pile.
With you and I both sorting,
we can do it with a smile."

"Oh, thank you," said the caterpillar.
"Come and have a seat.
Aren't you awfully glad that you
don't have so many feet?"

Fun With Fluency

1. How does the caterpillar feel in the last stanza?
bored   confused
grateful   frustrated

2. Without looking at the poem, write in the commas in the sentences below. Then look at the poem to check your work. Correct any mistakes.

Yellow socks and orange socks purple socks and green. Red and blue and pink ones too and striped ones in-between.

3. When reading this poem aloud, which words would you emphasize in the third stanza? Why?

_____

_____

_____

_____

_____

FLUENCY SPOTLIGHT

Dialogue, Exclamations, Typographical Signals

MEANING FIRST

Before the modeled reading, read aloud and discuss the passage. Pose this or another comprehension question: *Imagine that your mother and father brought home a baby brother who was really a baby seal. How do you think you'd react?* Now continue with the lesson and read the passage again with a focus on fluency.

MODEL AND DISCUSS FLUENCY

Proceed with a modeled reading of the excerpt from *Alligator Baby*. Emphasize the distinct character voices, exaggerate the exclamations, and stress the italicized word *not* in the middle of the passage. Use the script provided here as a sample for your own instructional dialogue with students.

Dialogue: *"As I read this text, you'll notice that I sound quite shocked and upset when I read Kirsten's words. Don't you think you'd be shocked and upset if your mom and dad brought home a baby seal instead of a baby brother? And if you were the dad, don't you think you might be quite shocked if your little baby reached up and flapped your face with a flipper? I read the words the way I think the characters would say them."*

Exclamations: *"The other reason why I read Kristen's words and the father's words in a shocked tone is because the author ended some of their sentences with exclamation points. The exclamation points tell us that the characters have strong emotions, so the words have to be read with a lot of energy. Listen as I read the father's reaction to the baby seal flapping his face as if the words end in a period: He yelled,* **"Aaaaaahhhhhaaaaa. It's a seal baby. We've got the wrong baby."** *It is hard to believe that the father is really shocked if we read the sentences as if they were statements and not exclamations."*

Typographical Signals: *"Here's another trick authors have to help make their character's words come alive. Look closely at this sentence: "That is* **not** *my baby brother!" Notice that the word* **not** *looks a little different than the other words. The author put this word in italics to let us know that we should read the word with more emphasis. Listen to the difference as I read the sentence first with the word* **not** *written in regular type, and then with the word written in italics. Which way sounds more natural?"*

ALL TOGETHER NOW

Begin with a choral reading of the excerpted text, pointing to the words on the transparency as the class follows along. Have Kristen's reaction gradually build in intensity, so her last line has real impact. Once the class is sufficiently comfortable with the text, have the class read just the dialogue of Kristen and the father, while you read the narration and the mother's dialogue.

Practice, Practice, Practice!

Partner Reading: Reading from their student copies, partners can break the text into parts as you did with the whole class. Partners switch parts when they feel they have reached a fluent level of reading. As always with partner reading, encourage students to gently support each other and offer guidance when needed.

Name: _____   Date: _____

Excerpt from **Alligator Baby**
by Robert Munsch

Kristen lifted up the bottom of the blanket, saw a fishy tail, and said, "That's not a people tail."

Kristen lifted up the middle of the blanket, saw a flipper, and said, "That's not a people flipper."

Kristen lifted up the top of the blanket, saw a face with whiskers, and said, "That's not a people face. That is *not* my baby brother!"

"Now, Kristen," said her mother, "don't be jealous."

Just then the baby reached up with its flipper and flapped her father's face: wap, wap, wap, wap, wap, wap, wap.

He yelled, "Aaaaaahhhhhaaaaa! It's a seal baby! We've got the wrong baby."

So Kristen put the seal baby in the bathtub, and her mother and father drove back to the zoo.

Fun With Fluency

Put a check next to the sentence in each pair that sounds most natural or believable.

1. ____ "Ouch. I've just been stung by a bee." cried Eddy.
   ____ "Ouch! I've just been stung by a bee!" cried Eddy.

2. ____ I am not going into that haunted house alone.
   ____ I am *not* going into that haunted house alone.

3. ____ As the first snow began to fall, the class shouted, "Yippee!"
   ____ As the first snow began to fall, the class shouted, "Yippee."

PART 3

Putting It All Together

FLUENCY SPOTLIGHT

Typographical Signals, Tone

MEANING FIRST

Before the modeled reading, read aloud and discuss the passage. Pose this or another discussion topic: *Discuss the author's purpose for writing this passage.* Now continue with the lesson and read the passage again with a focus on fluency.

MODEL AND DISCUSS FLUENCY

Proceed with a modeled reading. Begin by reading the title and telling (or reminding) students that Jane Yolen is a children's author and poet. As you read, stress the typographical signals, and note the thoughtful, peaceful tone of the second paragraph. Use the script provided here as a sample for your own instructional dialogue with students.

Typographical Signals: *"Did you notice in the first paragraph how I put extra emphasis on the word* **green**? *I did this because the author puts this word in quotation marks. She does this because in this case,* **green** *means something other than the color green, as she explains in the following sentence. There are also several words written in italics in this passage. In the first paragraph, italics are used to indicate the title of her book. In the second paragraph, she uses italics on* **swee-swash** *and* **kee-ya** *for emphasis. These words imitate the sounds they represent, and sound best if they are read with energy and expression."*

Tone: *"I love the rhythm of the second paragraph and the quiet, thoughtful mood. Notice how the author begins the sentences with verbs, beckoning the reader to* **feel**, **watch**, **listen**, *and* **become** *nature. I emphasize these words because that is how I think she would say them if she were here talking to us. Stressing these verbs also helps make the passage sound rhythmic. Now listen again as I read the short, dramatic sentences, followed by the two longer sentences. The commas in the last two sentences remind me to pause, and in this case, it is as if they are telling me to "Slow down and smell the roses!"*

ALL TOGETHER NOW

Do several choral readings of this passage. To make the reading more dramatic, try this variation: Divide the class into four groups and assign one of the last four sentences to each group. Read the passage in unison up to *Feel the grass . . .* and then have each group read their sentence.

Practice, Practice, Practice!

Taped Reading: Have students read the passage several times. Invite them to pretend they are Jane Yolen as they read. When they feel they are reading it fluently and with expression, have them record themselves while reading the passage. Encourage students to tape over their recording until they are satisfied with their reading. A partner can critique the tape and offer feedback.

Name: _____   Date: _____

A Writing Tip From Jane Yolen
by Jane Yolen

I think of myself as a "green" person. A "green" person is someone who loves nature. I have written many nature books. My book *Color Me a Rhyme* is a poetry book about nature's many colors.

Here's a writing tip: To write color poems, find something in nature. Go out and sit in a meadow or park. Feel the grass beneath you. Watch the sky overhead. Listen to the *swee-swash* of wind through reeds, the *kee-ya* of a hawk. Become a tree, a flower, a fern uncurling in spring.

Fun With Fluency

1. Are you a "green" person? Explain your answer.

_____

_____

_____

2. Choose a sentence from the passage that was read in a special way. Underline the sentence in the passage.

How was the sentence read in a special way?

_____

_____

Why was the sentence read in a special way?

_____

_____

FLUENCY SPOTLIGHT

Exclamations, Commas, Intonation

MEANING FIRST

Before the modeled reading, read aloud and discuss the chant. Explain that chants usually have strong rhythms. Talk about why "Togetherness Chant" is a good title for this chant. Brainstorm other suitable titles. Now continue with the lesson and read the chant again with a focus on fluency.

MODEL AND DISCUSS FLUENCY

Proceed with a modeled reading of "Togetherness Chant." Stress each exclamation, pause, and the rhythm of the chant. Use the script provided here as a sample for your own instructional dialogue with students.

Exclamations: *"Wow! Each sentence in the first two stanzas ends in an exclamation point. The poet really wants us to say these sentences with a lot of energy. And I can see why. Let's compare how these sentences sound if we read them as if they end in a period. The lines sound very dull, right?"*

Commas: *"Now look at all the commas the poet uses in the third and fourth stanzas. Commas are an important tool writers use to separate items in a list and keep them from running into each other. The commas also help create a strong rhythm in this chant. Listen as I read these stanzas and note the power of each and every pause."*

Intonation: *"In chants, certain words are strongly emphasized for dramatic effect. Listen as I read the first two stanzas. Which words do you hear me emphasize?* **We like pizza! We like toys! We like games with lots of noise!** *. . . Stressing the last word in each sentence helps gives this chant its rhythm.*

ALL TOGETHER NOW

Begin with a choral reading of "Togetherness Chant," pointing to each word as students follow along on the transparency. For a fun variation, divide the class in half and have the groups read alternate stanzas.

Practice, Practice, Practice!

Cross-Age Reading: A young audience will delight in listening to your students read the rhythmic "Togetherness Chant." Here's a challenge. Invite students to personalize their chant by adding their own names. Can they keep the rhythm and rhyme of the chant?

Name: _____   Date: _____

Togetherness Chant

(by Helen H. Moore from *A Poem a Day*)

We like pizza!
We like toys!
We like games
with lots of noise!

We like dogs!
We like cola!
We like chanting
our name-ola!

Hector, Nelson,
Kiko, Jane,
Michael, Justin,
Tasha, Zane,
Devon, Kevin,
Mallory, Zack—
Give me five
and I'll give it back!

Brandon, Keisha,
Darnell, Sue,
Hillary, Isaac,
Marcus, Lou.
Come play with us,
we'll play with you,
Together there's nothing
we can't do!

Fun With Fluency

1. How do you feel after reading "Together Chant"?

tired   frustrated

energized   bored

2. Underline the words that are emphasized when read aloud in the first two stanzas.

3. If you were to write a chant about the things that you and your friends like, what would you list in your chant?

_____

_____

_____

_____

_____

_____

FLUENCY SPOTLIGHT

PART 3

Putting It All Together

Dialogue

MEANING FIRST

Before the modeled reading, read aloud and discuss the passage. Pose these or other discussion topics: *How would you describe Nancy? Describe Jake's reaction to Nancy.* Now continue with the lesson and read the passage again with a focus on fluency.

MODEL AND DISCUSS FLUENCY

Proceed with a modeled reading of the excerpt from *Swamp Monster in Third Grade*, distinguishing each character's voice and tone. Use the script provided here as a sample for your own instructional dialogue with students.

Dialogue: *"How do we decide how to make characters sound when we read dialogue aloud? The best way is to think about the meaning of the words the character speaks. How do you think you would say those words if you were in the character's shoes? Or how do you think the character would say the words if they were able to speak for themselves? Sometimes, authors give us clues as to how to read a character's words. Let's look at the second paragraph after Nancy warns her brother that he's going to get in big trouble:* **"Get out of here and leave me alone," he snapped.** *The author could have written* **he said,** *but instead, she chose her words carefully and wrote,* **he snapped.** *That way, we know that Jake is irritated with his sister. A little further down we see that the author dropped another clue—the same clue, in fact, about how Jake is feeling:* **"I'm just looking," Jake snapped.** *I know that I'm going to read Jake's words with a frustrated and angry tone."*

ALL TOGETHER NOW

Do an echo reading of the passage, one to two sentences at a time. Contrast the different tones of each character's voice with the neutral tone of the narration.

Practice, Practice, Practice!

Trio Reading: In groups of three, have students read the parts of Nancy, Jake, and the narration. Remind students to say the words the way they think the character might say the words. Students rotate roles once they have achieved fluency. For additional support, color-code each part with highlighters.

Name: _____   Date: _____

Excerpt from Swamp Monster in Third Grade
by Debbie Dadey

"You're going to get in big trouble," Nancy told her brother.

Jake splashed swamp water at his sister with his green, webbed hand. "Get out of here and leave me alone," he snapped. Jake looked past the weeds and scraggly trees of the swamp to a nearby picnic area. Four human kids about his age were eating and drinking. Jake sighed. Something about humans had always fascinated him.

"You know you're not supposed to hang out near those webless creatures. Mom says nothing good can come from it," Nancy said, looking at the kids. They had finished their lunches and were tossing a brightly colored disk around.

"I'm just looking," Jake snapped.

Nancy used her tail to scratch her nose before answering. "You're going to get in trouble. Let's go home. I'm hungry. I bet Dad made a big pot of crawfish for lunch."

Fun With Fluency

Put a check next to the sentence in each pair that makes the most sense.

1. ☐ "I don't feel very good," laughed Justin.
   ☐ "I don't feel very good," moaned Justin.

2. ☐ "Watch out for the hole!" Susan yelled.
   ☐ "Watch out for the hole!" Susan whispered.

3. ☐ "I just want to be left alone," sang Doug.
   ☐ "I just want to be left alone," sneered Doug.

On the back of this page, draw your own swamp monster.

FLUENCY SPOTLIGHT

Pauses, Exclamations

MEANING FIRST

Before the modeled reading, read aloud and discuss the passage. Pose these or other comprehension questions: *Were you surprised by the facts presented in "Mighty Midgets"? What shocked you the most?* Now continue with the lesson and read the passage again with a focus on fluency.

MODEL AND DISCUSS FLUENCY

Proceed with a modeled reading of "Mighty Midgets," emphasizing the pauses and exclamations. Use the script provided here as a sample for your own instructional dialogue with students.

Pauses: *"Remember we said that an em dash signals a stronger pause than a comma. Look at the dash in the first sentence. Now listen as I read the sentence, and note the long pause after I read the word* **humans: Insects are much stronger than humans—for their size!** *I think the authors used a dash here because they want you to really think about that first statement, which is quite baffling. They want you to think, "No way are insects stronger than humans!" before they go on to explain how the statement is in fact true. The authors could have written,* **For their size, insects are much stronger than humans**, *but this way is not as suspenseful and exciting."*

Exclamations: *"Did you notice the way I read this passage with a sense of amazement? One reason is because the information is quite extraordinary. I also came across several exclamation points as I was reading, and those punctuation marks signaled me to read with a tone of astonishment:* **If you could do that, you'd be able to jump the length of two football fields!** *The information and the way the sentence is punctuated makes me think, 'Wow! That fact is truly amazing!'"*

ALL TOGETHER NOW

Do a choral reading of "Mighty Midgets," pointing to each word as you read from the transparency. Can students feel the sense of amazement behind the words?

Practice, Practice, Practice!

Partner Reading: After the class choral reading of "Mighty Midgets," partners can read from their student copies. As always with partner reading, encourage students to gently support each other and offer guidance when needed.

Name: _____   Date: _____

Mighty Midgets

(excerpted from *Flies Taste With Their Feet: Weird Facts About Insects*
by Melvin and Gilda Berger)

Insects are much stronger than humans—for their size!
An ant can lift a crumb 50 times as heavy as itself. If you
were as strong, you could carry a ton of bricks.

A *flea* can jump about 13 inches. If you could do that, you'd
be able to jump the length of two football fields!

Cockroaches can run about 2 and $\frac{1}{2}$ miles an hour.
At that rate, you could race along at 130 miles an hour!

Fun With Fluency

1. Which fact do you find the most amazing? Why?

_____

_____

_____

2. Write three facts that are so amazing, they should end in exclamation
points. (You can make up the facts if you'd like.)

1) _____

_____

2) _____

_____

3) _____

_____

Appendix
Phrased Text Lessons

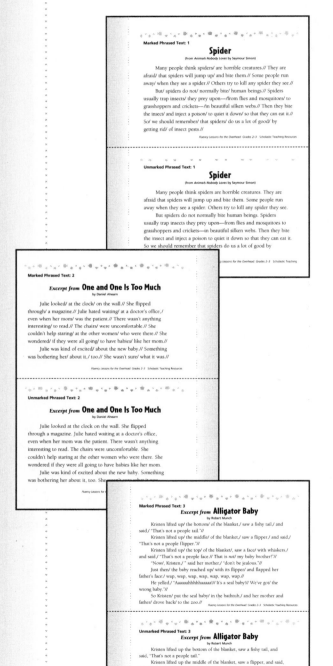

Watch / out! / That / cow / might / slime / you / with / its / long / tongue! Do you have students whose staccato, word-by-word reading has become a habit? These students put so much attention on decoding the words that there is little energy left over to focus on how the words relate to each other and the overall text. Even if the students are reading the words accurately, their comprehension is in jeopardy because they are not grouping the words into meaningful phrases. It is often the phrases that hold the meaning, rather than individual words. These students need explicit instruction in chunking written words into meaningful segments. One way to do this is through the Phrased Text Lesson (PTL) (Rasinski, 1994; 2003).

The PTL provides students with actual cues (slashes) embedded in the text that signal to the reader when to pause. A single slash at the end of a phrase break indicates a short pause, while a double slash at the end of a sentence indicates a longer pause: Watch out! // That cow / might slime you / with its long tongue! // Modeling how to phrase text with tangible cues is an effective strategy for improving students' phrasing and overall reading (Rasinski, 1990; 1994).

On page 51 is Rasinski's (2003) step-by-step Phrased Text Lesson. He recommends approximately hundred-word reading passages or segments from texts that students have recently read or will read in the near future.

Use the phrased reading passages on pages 52–54 along with the guidelines.

Phrased Text Lesson: A Quick Guide

The PTL is designed to be taught to individual students or small groups, over two consecutive days, 10 to 15 minutes each day.

Day 1

1. Give each student a copy of a phrase-cued text, (such as those found on pages 52 to 54.)

2. Remind students of the importance of reading in phrases, not word by word.

3. Explain the purpose of phrase markings on the text.

4. Read the text to students several times, emphasizing and slightly exaggerating the phrases.

5. Read the text with students two or three times in a choral fashion, emphasizing good phrasing and expression.

6. Have students read the text orally with a partner, two or three readings per student.

7. Have students perform the text orally for the group.

Day 2

Repeat the procedure from the first day, using the same text *without the phrase boundaries* marked to help students transfer their understanding of phrased reading to conventional text.

(Excerpted from *The Fluent Reader* by Timothy Rasinski, Scholastic, 2003)

Spider

(from *Animals Nobody Loves* by Seymour Simon)

Many people think spiders/ are horrible creatures.// They are afraid/ that spiders will jump up/ and bite them.// Some people run away/ when they see a spider.// Others try to kill any spider they see.//

But/ spiders do not/ normally bite/ human beings.// Spiders usually trap insects/ they prey upon—/from flies and mosquitoes/ to grasshoppers and crickets—/in beautiful silken webs.// Then they bite the insect/ and inject a poison/ to quiet it down/ so that they can eat it.// So/ we should remember/ that spiders/ do us a lot of good/ by getting rid/ of insect pests.//

Spider

(from *Animals Nobody Loves* by Seymour Simon)

Many people think spiders are horrible creatures. They are afraid that spiders will jump up and bite them. Some people run away when they see a spider. Others try to kill any spider they see.

But spiders do not normally bite human beings. Spiders usually trap insects they prey upon—from flies and mosquitoes to grasshoppers and crickets—in beautiful silken webs. Then they bite the insect and inject a poison to quiet it down so that they can eat it. So we should remember that spiders do us a lot of good by getting rid of insect pests.

Excerpt from **One and One Is Too Much**
by Daniel Ahearn

Julie looked/ at the clock/ on the wall.// She flipped through/ a magazine.// Julie hated waiting/ at a doctor's office,/ even when her mom/ was the patient.// There wasn't anything interesting/ to read.// The chairs/ were uncomfortable.// She couldn't help staring/ at the other women/ who were there.// She wondered/ if they were all going/ to have babies/ like her mom.//

Julie was kind of excited/ about the new baby.// Something was bothering her/ about it,/ too.// She wasn't sure/ what it was.//

Unmarked Phrased Text: 2

Excerpt from **One and One Is Too Much**
by Daniel Ahearn

Julie looked at the clock on the wall. She flipped through a magazine. Julie hated waiting at a doctor's office, even when her mom was the patient. There wasn't anything interesting to read. The chairs were uncomfortable. She couldn't help staring at the other women who were there. She wondered if they were all going to have babies like her mom.

Julie was kind of excited about the new baby. Something was bothering her about it, too. She wasn't sure what it was.

Marked Phrased Text: 3

Excerpt from **Alligator Baby**
by Robert Munsch

Kristen lifted up/ the bottom/ of the blanket,/ saw a fishy tail,/ and said,/ "That's not a people tail."//

Kristen lifted up/ the middle/ of the blanket,/ saw a flipper,/ and said,/ "That's not a people flipper."//

Kristen lifted up/ the top/ of the blanket,/ saw a face/ with whiskers,/ and said,/ "That's not a people face.// That is *not*/ my baby brother!"//

"Now/, Kristen,"/ said her mother,/ "don't be jealous."//

Just then/ the baby reached up/ with its flipper/ and flapped her father's face:/ wap, wap, wap, wap, wap, wap, wap.//

He yelled,/ "Aaaaaahhhhhaaaaa!// It's a seal baby!// We've got/ the wrong baby."//

So Kristen/ put the seal baby/ in the bathtub,/ and her mother and father/ drove back/ to the zoo.//

Fluency Lessons for the Overhead: Grades 2–3   Scholastic Teaching Resources

---

Unmarked Phrased Text: 3

Excerpt from **Alligator Baby**
by Robert Munsch

Kristen lifted up the bottom of the blanket, saw a fishy tail, and said, "That's not a people tail."

Kristen lifted up the middle of the blanket, saw a flipper, and said, "That's not a people flipper."

Kristen lifted up the top of the blanket, saw a face with whiskers, and said, "That's not a people face. That is *not* my baby brother!""Now, Kristen," said her mother, "don't be jealous." Just then the baby reached up with its flipper and flapped her father's face: wap, wap, wap, wap, wap, wap, wap.

He yelled, "Aaaaaahhhhhaaaaa! It's a seal baby! We've got the wrong baby."

So Kristen put the seal baby in the bathtub, and her mother and father drove back to the zoo.

Fluency Lessons for the Overhead: Grades 2–3   Scholastic Teaching Resources

Bibliography

Professional

Allington, R.L. "Fluency: The Neglected Reading Goal." *The Reading Teacher*, 36, 556–561. 1983.

Nathan, R.G. and K.E. Stanovich. "The Causes and Consequences of Differences in Reading Fluency." *Theory Into Practice*. 30 (1991): 176–184 (1991).

National Reading Panel. "Report of the National Reading Panel: Teaching Children to Read." Report of the Subgroups. Washington, DC: U.S. Department of Health and Human Services, National Institutes of Health, 2000.

Rasinski, T.V. "Developing Syntactic Sensitivity in Reading Through Phrase-Cued Texts." *Intervention in School and Clinic*. 29, No. 3 (January 1994).

Rasinski, T.V. "The Effects of Cued Phrase Boundaries in Texts." Bloomington, IN: ERIC Clearinghouse on Reading and Communication Skills (ED 313 689), 1990.

Rasinski, T.V. *The Fluent Reader: Oral Reading Strategies for Building Word Recognition, Fluency, and Comprehension*. New York: Scholastic, 2003.

Snow, C. E., S. M. Burns, and P. Griffin. (Eds.). *Preventing Reading Difficulties in Young Children*. Washington, DC: National Academy Press, 1998.

Wolf, M. and T. Katzir-Cohen. "Reading Fluency and Its Intervention." *Scientific Studies of Reading* (Special Issue on Fluency. Editors: E. Kameenui & D. Simmons). 5 (2001): 211–238.

Reading Passages

"Spider" from *Animals Nobody Loves* by Seymour Simon (Chronicle Books, 2001)

"Twist and Turn!" from *Weather or Not* by Maryann Dobeck (Scholastic, 2002)

One and One Is Too Much by Daniel Ahearn (Scholastic, 2002)

"Untitled Chant" from *Writing Funny Bone Poems* by Paul Janeczko
(Scholastic, 2001)

"Eyeballs for Sale!" from *A Pizza the Size of the Sun* by Jack Prelutsky
(HarperCollins, 1996)

"What If?" by Helen H. Moore from *A Poem a Day* (Scholastic, 2000)

"Mix-Up" by Andrea Martin from *Kids' Poems: Teaching Third & Fourth Graders
to Love Writing Poetry* by Regie Routman (Scholastic, 2000)

Hey, Little Ant by Phillip and Hannah Hoose (Tricycle Press, 1998)

Listening to Whales Sing by Faith McNulty (Scholastic, 1996)

"At the Laundry" from *Poems to Count On* by Sandra Liatsos (Scholastic, 1995)

Alligator Baby by Robert Munsch (Scholastic, 1997)

"A Writing Tip From Jane Yolen" by Jane Yolen from *Scholastic News*.
Edition 2 (2001).

"Togetherness Chant" by Helen H. Moore from *A Poem a Day* (Scholastic, 2000)

Swamp Monster in Third Grade by Debbie Dadey (Scholastic, 2002)

"Mighty Midgets" from *Flies Taste With Their Feet: Weird Facts About Insects*
by Melvin and Gilda Berger (Scholastic, 1997)